IN COLOR

THE 1970s

STEPHEN FEINSTEIN

Library of Congress Cataloging-in-Publication Data

Feinstein, Stephen.
    The 1970s from Watergate to Disco / Stephen Feinstein.—
        Rev. ed.
        p. cm. — (Decades of the 20th century in color)
    Includes index.
        ISBN-10: 0-7660-2637-X
        1. Nineteen seventies—Juvenile literature. 2. United
    States—History—1969- —Juvenile literature. 3. Popular
    culture—United States—History—20th century—Juvenile
    literature. 4. United States—Social life and customs—1971–
    —Juvenile literature. I. Title. II. Series.

    E839.F35 2006
    973.924—dc22
                                        2005019874

ISBN-13: 978-0-7660-2637-7

Printed in the United States of America

10 9 8 7 6 5 4 3

To Our Readers: We have done our best to make sure all Internet addresses in this book were active and appropriate when we went to press. However, the author and the publisher have no control over and assume no liability for the material available on those Internet sites or on other Web sites they may link to. Any comments or suggestions can be sent by e-mail to comments@enslow.com or to the address on the back cover.

Illustration Credits: AP/ Wide World Photos, pp. 4, 8, 12, 14, 15, 16, 26, 27, 28, 30, 31, 32, 35, 39, 45, 46, 49, 51, 56, 57, 58; Corel Corporation, p. 10; Enslow Publishers, Inc., pp. 7, 20; Everett Collection, Inc., pp. 21, 22, 23; National Aeronautics and Space Administration (NASA), pp. 52, 54, 55; The Jimmy Carter Library, p. 41; JupiterImages Corporation, pp. 6, 17, 24, 43; Library of Congress, p. 34; National Archives, p. 37.

All interior collages composed by Enslow Publishers, Inc. Images used are courtesy of the previously credited rights holders, above.

Cover Illustrations: AP/ Wide World Photos; JupiterImages Corporation.

Contents

The 1970s opened with the United States still reeling from the protests and dissension over the Vietnam War. Below, a group of Vietnam veterans leave their medals and ribbons at the front of the Capitol Building.

Introduction

As the United States entered the 1970s, the nation was in turmoil.
America was still involved in a war in Vietnam, which many saw as a
tragic mistake. Many took to the streets in protest. By the mid-1970s,
America had managed to get out of the war, but the deep divisions it
had caused would take many years to heal.

Around the same time, Americans learned that President Richard
Nixon had authorized a coverup of his administration's involvement in
the Watergate affair—an illegal break-in at the headquarters of the
Democratic National Committee. This led many to lose trust in their
political leaders.

Many Americans stopped getting involved in politics. People
were bitter and exhausted. Many began to focus more on their own
problems and needs. Young people who had become hippies in the
1960s looked for ways to rejoin the mainstream. They started to
build careers and seek financial success.

Writer Tom Wolfe noticed that Americans were becoming more
preoccupied with their own well-being. They were concerned with
eating healthful foods and looking good. In 1976, Wolfe described
the 1970s as the "Me Decade."

The Counterculture

Although the 1960s had been marked by upheaval—struggles for civil rights, the anti-Vietnam war movement, and urban rioting—that decade had been a period when many Americans were well-off financially.

Good economic conditions made it easy for young people to put off decisions about careers and marriage. Housing, food, and energy were cheap. A youth "counterculture" sprang up to protest

any kind of limits on personal freedoms. Young people felt free to question the traditional values of their parents and government and religious leaders. The baby boom that took place after World War II created an enormous population of young people. Four out of ten Americans in the mid-1960s were under the age of seventeen. It is no wonder they were able to cause such a stir.

Members of the counterculture were often referred to as "hippies." The main goal for many was to oppose the war in Vietnam. Others, not so focused on politics, also rejected traditional values. Sex, drugs, and rock 'n' roll were important elements of the hippie lifestyle. Hippies also experimented with various types of communal living arrangements.

Many men grew their hair long. The use of drugs, such as marijuana and LSD, increased dramatically. People became much more tolerant of sexual experimentation. It seemed to many that "free love" could become a part of everyday life.

Taking the "Counter" Out of "Counterculture"

In the 1970s, the economy went through some drastic changes. Life became more difficult. Many people had trouble making ends meet. Dropping out of the mainstream no longer seemed to be a wise option. Young people once again became concerned with making the right career decisions.

By the second half of the 1970s, however, it was clear that certain aspects of the youth counterculture had become part of mainstream culture. Rock 'n' roll had become a multibillion-dollar consumer business. It was now just as big a part of the American capitalist system as any other industry.

Black Pride

The civil rights movement led to a growing sense of ethnic pride among the various ethnic groups in the United States in the 1970s. African Americans focused on their African cultural

In the 1970s, many people felt more free to do what came naturally, without worrying much about what others would think. Fashions, hairstyles (left), and attitudes toward drugs and sex were all affected by this newfound American freedom, which had begun to take root among the hippies in the 1960s.

During the 1960s, African Americans had waged and won a battle for civil rights. In the 1970s, other groups, such as women and the Hispanic-American farm workers led by Cesar Chavez (above), would start their own struggles for equality.

heritage. They adopted African styles of fashion along with an awareness that "black is beautiful." African-American men wore their hair in natural Afro styles. African-American women wore brightly colored, loose-fitting garments known as *dashikis*.

In 1977, a television miniseries based on Alex Haley's book *Roots* was broadcast. *Roots* told the story of Alex Haley's family history in America, beginning with Kunta Kinte, who had been brought from Africa to work as a slave in Virginia in 1767. About 130 million Americans tuned in each night to follow the story of the succeeding generations of the Haley family.

Roots inspired pride in African Americans. But it also influenced members of other ethnic groups. All of a sudden, everyone seemed interested in learning about his or her own ethnic background. People joined ethnic political organizations and participated in ethnic neighborhood celebrations. Colleges and schools offered courses in ethnic studies. And with a little bit of research, it soon became apparent that all people, no matter what their ethnicity, had good reason to feel proud.

Hispanic-American Pride

Millions of Hispanic Americans took pride in the heroic work of Cesar Chavez, the leader of the United Farm Workers Union. He used nonviolent tactics to gain better working conditions for farmworkers. He successfully organized sit-ins, picket lines, and consumer boycotts to win a bitter strike against California grape growers. In 1979, he led an eight-month strike against California lettuce growers.

Meanwhile, a Hispanic-American political group called La Raza Unida in East Los Angeles and the Southwest organized Hispanic-American workers to promote better working conditions and higher wages. And Spanish-language news-papers and Hispanic television stations also contributed to a growing sense of pride on the part of Hispanic Americans in their own culture.

American Indian Movement

American Indians, too, were inspired by this new sense of ethnic pride. Their main concern was to protect their lands from further seizure by the federal or state governments. In 1972, about five hundred members of the American Indian Movement (AIM) seized the Bureau of Indian Affairs in

Washington, D.C., to protest treaty violations. They occupied the building for a week. This action spurred the government to make changes at the bureau and to begin to address the Indians' grievances.

In 1973, AIM protested unfair treatment of Indians by law officers at the Pine Ridge Reservation at Wounded Knee, South Dakota, the scene of a massacre of Indians by the United States Army in 1890. AIM's protests led to a two-month-long confrontation between Indians and police. The actions of AIM contributed to a growing sense of American Indian pride. The following year, Indians gained the right to control federal aid for education and other services on their reservations with the Indian Self-Determination Act of 1974.

American Indians continued to come under pressure from energy companies who wanted to drill for natural gas and mine coal and uranium on Indian lands. The courts granted Indians the right to negotiate their own contracts with energy companies. But in some places the activities of the energy companies disturbed the Indians' sacred burial grounds. Uranium mining and coal-burning power plants in particular caused environmental pollution on Indian lands. To protest such activities and draw attention to the situation, Indians in 1978 organized a peaceful demonstration called The Longest Walk. Indian activists walked three-thousand miles from San Francisco to Washington, D.C., a walk that took five months to complete.

Gurus and Cults

The 1970s were a confusing time for many people. Those who had questioned traditional beliefs during the 1960s now needed to find something else in which to believe. Many were drawn to gurus, or spiritual guides, from India. Gurus were eager to train new disciples in various Indian religious or mystical traditions. Maharishi Mahesh Yogi became widely popular after the Beatles and other celebrities became followers. The Maharishi even appeared as a guest on Johnny Carson's *Tonight Show*.

A group of people dressed in robes and chanting "Hare Krishna" became a common sight at airports and on busy downtown streets all around the country. These people were followers of a guru known as Swami A. C. Bhaktivedanta.

People from many different religious traditions attracted groups of devoted followers. In some cases, cult members were brainwashed. The Reverend Sun Myung Moon, a South

The women's liberation movement, which included speeches and rallies (below), was one of the broadest and most successful such movements in American history.

Korean Presbyterian minister, attracted a huge following of young people to his Unification Church. His followers came to be called "Moonies."

The People's Temple cult came to a bizarre and tragic end in the 1970s. It was founded by Jim Jones, a Pentecostal minister, in 1955. In 1976, Jones relocated his one-thousand-person congregation to a place in the jungles of Guyana that he called the Promised Land, which then became known as Jonestown. Isolated from the rest of the world, Jones began to preach to his followers that disaster was coming. In 1978, California Congressman Leo Ryan visited Jonestown to investigate conditions there, at the request of families of cult members. As Ryan was leaving, he, along with several People's Temple members who were trying to leave Jonestown, was murdered by Jones's followers. After the killings, Jones and more than nine hundred of his followers took part in a mass suicide by drinking poisoned Kool-Aid.

Women's Liberation

Women were a major force for change in America in the 1970s. Throughout the decade, increasing numbers of feminists struggled for equal rights and an end to discrimination against women. They pressed for better educational opportunities, and as a result, Ivy League universities began to admit women as students. During the 1970s, there was a 500 percent increase in the number of women entering law schools. Forty percent of those entering medical schools were women, and 25 percent of doctorate degrees were earned by women.

Many types of jobs became available to women for the first time in the 1970s. Pat Schroeder, Elizabeth Holtzman, Barbara Jordan, and Bella Abzug were elected to serve in Congress.

The first two female United States Army generals were appointed in 1970, and the FBI hired its first female agents—Joanne Pierce and Susan Roley—in 1972. Also in 1972, Gloria Steinem published the first issue of *Ms.* magazine, a publication that dealt with feminist issues. Feminists believed that the term *Ms.* was preferable to *Miss* and *Mrs.* because women, just like men, should not have to be identified according to their marital status.

Designer Jeans

Young men and women in the early 1970s continued to wear the ragged denim blue jeans or army fatigues, cotton T-shirts, and long hair popular in the late 1960s. Often their blue jeans were decorated with peace symbols. Many young women, aiming for a natural look, did not use makeup or lipstick. The word *unisex* was often used to describe this generation's antifashion approach to dress.

But some people wanted to stand out from the crowd. For them, designers such as Calvin Klein created special blue jeans decorated with rhinestones or silver studs. Some came with matching jackets. Sold in high-fashion boutiques, the so-called designer jeans were very expensive.

Doing Your Own Thing

The "do-your-own-thing" philosophy of the 1960s counterculture had a big influence on the fashion of the 1970s. An amazing variety of styles was available. Women could choose

Fashions of the 1970s varied greatly. While young people still wore the ragged, used jeans popular in the 1960s, many others wore flashy designer clothes. Denim and flannel clothes (below) were also popular.

the supershort miniskirt of the 1960s, the longer hemline of the midiskirt, or long peasant skirts. These were sometimes worn with drawstring blouses, vests, and boots to create a western look.

Women also wore all kinds of pants, from velvet hot pants to tailored pants with a short jacket. Hot pants were tight-fitting, extremely short shorts. A typical winter look was hot pants and long boots beneath an overcoat. Many companies did not allow their female employees to wear hot pants to work. By the late 1970s, a more conventional feminine look became popular again. Women wore long graceful skirts, printed shawls, sundresses, and elegant evening wear.

One of the most popular and memorable looks of the 1970s was the broad silhouette of bell-bottom pants (above right). Bell-bottoms could be seen in the form of the tattered jeans worn by young people, as well as in the styles sold by leading designers.

The white leisure suit worn by John Travolta in the hit movie *Saturday Night Fever* (above) was perhaps the most iconic attire of the 1970s.

Polyester and Bell-Bottoms

In the mid-1970s, menswear entered a "peacock period." Brightly colored polyester leisure wear with purple, rose, orange, and green patterns became popular. Influenced by the dress styles of rock musicians, some men and women took to wearing platform shoes. The heels of these shoes could be as high as seven inches. Various kinds of leisure clothes also became popular. On the weekends, many men wore jogging suits—even those who had never jogged in their lives, and had no intention of ever jogging.

Another new leisure fashion look emerged from the disco scene. Discotheques—disco dance clubs—had appeared in cities all over the country, and people flocked to them. Many people were influenced by the disco fashion styles seen in the 1977 movie *Saturday Night Fever*, starring John Travolta. Men and women wore sexy, formfitting clothes. Men wore polyester shirts with colorful patterns and light-colored jackets with matching bell-bottom pants.

"Breaker, Breaker!"

Someone wishing to transmit a message over a CB (citizen band) radio would begin his or her broadcast with the words "breaker, breaker." In the mid-1970s, millions of Americans were uttering these words. People used their CB radios to contact other CB radio operators within a range of about four to five miles. CB radios first became available in 1947, but did not become popular until 1973. That was the year the federal government mandated a national speed limit of 55 miles per hour. Long-distance truckers tried to get around this new law by using CB radios to warn each other of the whereabouts of "Smokies" (highway police officers). Once the media began reporting the truckers' use of CBs and the colorful jargon they used in their broadcasts, millions of people all around the country rushed out to buy CBs. Even First Lady Betty Ford owned a CB and transmitted broadcasts under the name "First Mama." At the height of the CB craze in 1976, $1 billion worth of CBs were sold. But interest in CB radios faded away just as quickly as it had arisen. By the end of the decade, sales of CBs had plummeted.

CB radios (above) enjoyed a brief run of popularity in the mid-1970s. Thanks partly to Burt Reynolds and the film *Smokey and the Bandit*, people decided to try their luck at making contact with other highway drivers over CB radios, while keeping on the lookout for "Smokies."

Getting in Touch With Your Feelings

For Americans who were turning inward in 1975, what better way to explore their own feelings than to wear a mood ring? Millions of Americans, including Hollywood stars such as Sophia Loren and Paul Newman, did just that. The original mood stone ring was created and sold by Joshua Reynolds. Soon dozens of imitators began selling products with such names as "impulse ring" and "persona ring." Mood rings were available in every price range from $2 to $250.

The mood stone was made of liquid crystals encased within clear quartz. The stone was able to change its color, supposedly to show the mood of the person wearing the ring. For example, blue indicated happy feelings and reddish brown indicated feelings of insecurity. The liquid crystals were heat sensitive and actually responded to changes in body temperature, not mood.

A Pet That Required Little Training

In 1975, more than a million Americans spent four dollars each to buy a most unusual pet—a pet rock! Gary Dahl placed smooth, egg-shaped stones in boxes designed by a friend. Here was the perfect pet—one that did not make a mess, did not need special training, and did not need to be fed. Dahl said that Americans were tired of all the troubles in the world. They needed a good laugh, and that is precisely what the pet rock provided.

California Cuisine

Health-conscious Americans had a brand-new cuisine to enjoy in the 1970s. Alice Waters opened her Chez Panisse restaurant in Berkeley, California, in 1971. She developed an imaginative new approach to cooking based on the use of the freshest and purest ingredients. Many of the foods were grown in her own garden and on local farms and ranches. Waters's restaurant became very popular with diners and remains so to this day. Her healthful and nutritious style of food preparation soon became known as California cuisine. Dishes were put together with creative combinations of ingredients that were chosen to enhance natural flavors, such as black and white sesame seed seared ahi tuna with hot and sour raspberry sauce. Meats, fish, and poultry were typically seared on a grill to lock in the flavors and keep the food moist and tender. Before long, California cuisine began appearing in other parts of the country as well.

Biggest Movie Hits

Among the blockbuster hits of the 1970s were George Lucas's *Star Wars* (1977), Steven Spielberg's *Jaws* (1975), and *Close Encounters of the Third Kind* (1977). These were big-budget films that used daring new special effects. Another popular hit was *Grease* (1978), which evoked nostalgia for the supposedly simpler time of the 1950s. *Superman: The Movie* (1978) and *Rocky* (1976), two other big movies of the 1970s, were stories about heroes. In very different ways, these films were about good guys fighting bad guys and winning. Along with *Star Wars*, these films focused on a search for a hero, something that seemed to be missing in American life.

Popular Television Shows

Many of the television shows of the 1970s reflected nostalgia for earlier decades. Such TV shows included *Happy Days* and *Laverne and Shirley*, which fondly remembered the 1950s, and *Little House on the Prairie* and *The Waltons*, which celebrated the simple pleasures of frontier living.

One television show of the 1970s, however, dared to confront modern problems. Norman Lear's sitcom *All in the Family*, about the bigoted character Archie Bunker, dealt with issues such as racial prejudice, abortion, and feminism. *All in the Family* showed how families coped with such issues. But it usually did so in a comical way.

The Thrill Is Gone

By the early to mid-1970s, it was apparent that the counterculture's greatest days had passed. The music scene in the 1970s was filled with tragic events and disappointing developments, such as the breakup of the Beatles. In 1970, music fans were shocked to learn that legendary superstars Janis Joplin and Jimi Hendrix had died from drug overdoses. Jim Morrison, the lead singer of the Doors, died in 1971, also possibly from a drug overdose. In 1974, Cass Elliott of the Mamas and the Papas died. In 1977, Elvis Presley, "The King of Rock 'n' Roll," died.

Other film franchises that got their start in the seventies were *Rocky* and *Superman* (above).

The effect of the deaths of these famous musicians was greater than the passing of any one individual. Part of the effect was a loss of the energy and excitement that had drawn together a whole generation during the decade before.

New Styles of Music

As people of the 1970s turned inward and focused on their own pursuits, some music seemed to reflect this phenomenon. People responded enthusiastically to the mellow, laid-back music of artists such as James Taylor, Barry Manilow, John Denver, Linda Ronstadt, Barbra Streisand, Anne Murray, and Carly Simon. These artists sang tunes about love and loss on a personal level instead of a broad political level as many of their predecessors in the 1960s had done.

Some higher-energy groups and individual artists, however, continued to attract a devoted following. Among them were the Rolling Stones, the Who, the Grateful Dead, Bruce Springsteen, and Aerosmith. Groups such as Led Zeppelin, featuring loud and fast guitar work, were called heavy metal groups.

A kind of folk rock, played by such stars as Bob Dylan, Joni Mitchell, Paul Simon, and Billy

The 1970s were a time of tragedy for the world of music. Several popular stars died, many of them from drug overdoses, including Jimi Hendrix (below).

Joel, which focused on real life issues and hardships, was also popular during the 1970s.

Black soul music, which had attracted many fans during the 1960s, continued to be very popular in the 1970s. Aretha Franklin, Al Green, Marvin Gaye, Stevie Wonder, Gladys Knight and the Pips, the Jackson Five, and Smokey Robinson and the Miracles, were among the biggest soul stars.

Other types of music also became popular during the 1970s. Jamaican musicians such as Bob Marley and Jimmy Cliff created a style of music known as reggae. Jazz musicians such as Miles Davis, Chick Corea, and Herbie Hancock created a jazz-rock type of music. It featured extensive use of newly available electronic instruments.

"Shake Your Booty"

Perhaps the biggest new trend in music in the 1970s was disco, which appeared in the middle of the decade. Disco music featured a steady pulsing beat and catchy tunes. Lyrics

The premature deaths of so many famous singers, such as Janis Joplin (above), made many people wonder whether the freedom and the relaxed attitude toward drugs that had begun in the 1960s had gone too far.

Discotheques (above) were known for their colorful atmosphere, which often included strobe lights, mirror balls, and fog machines.

focused on love, sex, and the excitement of disco dancing. The disco style avoided the heavy topics of politics and hardship that had been popular in the 1960s. Disco was great for dancing and offered a temporary escape into fantasy and sensuality for millions of Americans who were ready for just that. The wild styles and carefree attitudes associated with disco appealed to young Americans, who were tired of the years of political and social protest of the 1960s and early 1970s. Donna Summer, whose career took off after the success of her sexy hit "Love to Love You Baby," was one of the most popular disco artists. In 1978, at the height of the disco craze, 36 million Americans danced the night away to the driving disco beat and flashing lights in twenty thousand discotheques (disco clubs) all around the country.

Getting Serious About Women's Tennis

In 1966, Billie Jean King won the singles tennis title in the women's division at the Wimbledon Championship Tournament in England. She was stunned when she was handed her prize—a gift certificate for clothes. In 1970, she was the women's division winner of the Open Tennis Tournament in Rome, where her $600 prize was considerably less than the $7,500 awarded to the winner of the men's division. Then in 1972 at the U.S. Open, she won $10,000 while men's champion Ilie Nastase won $25,000.

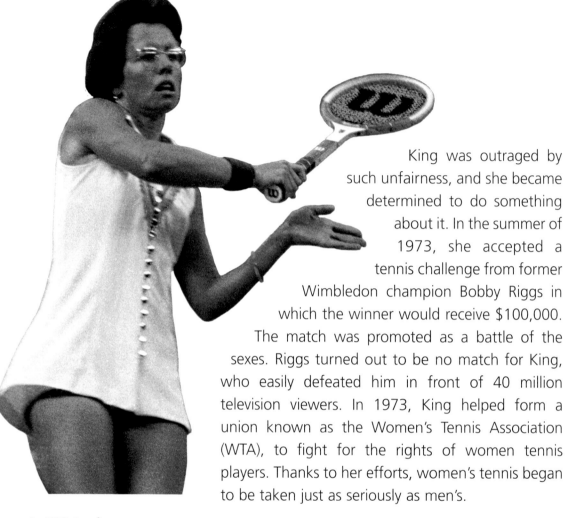

King was outraged by such unfairness, and she became determined to do something about it. In the summer of 1973, she accepted a tennis challenge from former Wimbledon champion Bobby Riggs in which the winner would receive $100,000. The match was promoted as a battle of the sexes. Riggs turned out to be no match for King, who easily defeated him in front of 40 million television viewers. In 1973, King helped form a union known as the Women's Tennis Association (WTA), to fight for the rights of women tennis players. Thanks to her efforts, women's tennis began to be taken just as seriously as men's.

In 1973, tennis star Billie Jean King (above) took women's liberation a big step forward when she defeated the male champion Bobby Riggs in what was called the "Battle of the Sexes."

Arthur Ashe—Tennis Champ

On July 5, 1975, tennis player Arthur Ashe became the first African American to win the Wimbledon men's singles tournament. Throughout his career, Ashe had faced racial discrimination. He had developed his talents playing in the segregated parks in his hometown of Richmond, Virginia. When he beat tennis pro Jimmy Connors at Wimbledon in 1975, Ashe made great strides toward breaking the color barrier in professional tennis.

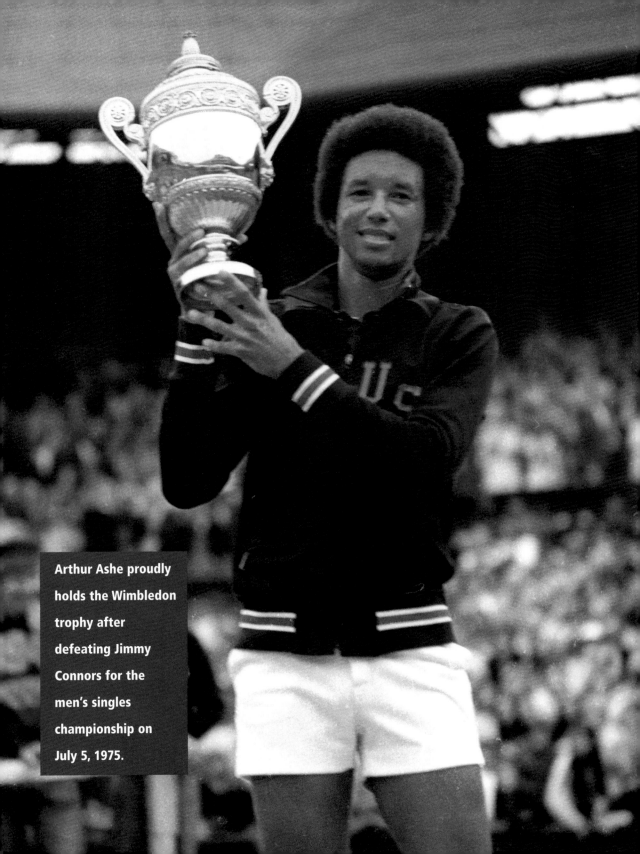

Arthur Ashe proudly holds the Wimbledon trophy after defeating Jimmy Connors for the men's singles championship on July 5, 1975.

Tensions and violence had been going on in the Middle East for decades. But in 1972, the violence spread to an unlikely place—the Olympics. Palestinian terrorists took several members of the Israeli Olympic team hostage, to show their desire to create a separate homeland for Palestinians in Israel. The standoff, which involved sharpshooters working their way over the rooftops of the Olympic Village (above), eventually resulted in the murder of all nine Israeli hostages.

Olympic Jewish Massacre

Political turmoil and violence had plagued the Middle East for decades. The main conflict was the struggle between Israel and its Arab neighbors. The Jewish people of Israel and the Arabs who lived in surrounding nations were frequently at odds over the issue of who was the rightful owner of the Holy Land, a territory with great religious meaning for Jews, Muslims, and Christians. Acts of terrorism were frequent. But in the 1970s, this unrest affected more than politics. In September 1972, Palestinian terrorists climbed into the compound housing athletes at the Olympic Games in Munich, Germany. They stormed the building where the athletes from Israel were staying, killing two Israeli Olympic team members and taking nine others hostage. After negotiations for the hostages' release went awry, all nine hostages, along with five of the terrorists, were shot and killed. The tragic terrorist attack shocked sports fans and millions of others around the world.

The Fighter Who Had a Way With Words

"Float like a butterfly, sting like a bee," was one of the ways Muhammad Ali described his boxing technique. Born Cassius Clay, Ali referred to himself as "the Greatest." As heavyweight champion in the 1960s, he had spoken out against the war in Vietnam. As a Black Muslim, Ali refused to be drafted into the army, and he was convicted of draft evasion. His license to box and his title were taken away from him. But in 1970, the United States Supreme Court overturned the ruling. Before long, Ali was back in the ring. After several tough bouts, he regained his title in a fight called "The Rumble in the Jungle" against George Foreman in 1974.

Muhammad Ali (right) was one of the most famous sports figures of the 1970s. In addition to boxing, Ali was a poet and an antiwar activist, whose protests against the draft got him into trouble in the 1960s.

Evel Knievel: America's Legendary Daredevil

Perhaps the most unusual sports figure of the 1970s was Evel Knievel. Known as America's Legendary Daredevil, Knievel became famous for his amazing, death-defying stunts. Among his best-known stunts were his motorcycle jumps over multiple cars and buses, which he continued despite several serious crashes and injuries. In October 1975, Knievel successfully jumped his motorcycle over fourteen Greyhound buses in Ohio. Like many of his other feats, this performance was televised and some 52 percent of Americans were watching as Knievel performed his latest stunt.

Evel Knievel sought to break records with his death-defying feats, such as his 3/4-mile rocket jump over Snake River Canyon in Idaho in 1974 (above).

Troops patrol a plantation during a seek-and-destroy mission to locate Viet Cong near Ben-Cat in 1970.

Ending the Vietnam War

President Lyndon Johnson announced that he would not run for re-election in 1968. He knew that the voters would not re-elect him. They blamed him for the long war in Vietnam, which was being fought to keep the Communist North Vietnamese from taking over South Vietnam. In 1968, the Vietnam War had become America's longest war. And it would last until 1975.

Richard Nixon was the Republican presidential candidate. He told the American people what they wanted to hear. Nixon promised to end the war "with honor," and to bring Americans together—to heal the divisions in American society caused by the war. Nixon narrowly defeated Hubert Humphrey in the 1968 election. By the time he was inaugurated, many American people were voicing opposition to the war. He knew that the longer the war dragged on, the more difficult it would be to accomplish anything else. His military advisors said that it could take many more years to win the war, and it would require larger numbers of American troops. The American people would not stand for this.

The North Vietnamese, led by Ho Chi Minh (above), fought with determination to unite Vietnam under Communism.

Nixon and his advisors briefly considered using nuclear weapons to end the war quickly. This, however, appeared too risky. Nixon also knew, as Johnson had, that to withdraw suddenly from the war in an obvious defeat, would be political suicide. So Nixon decided on a plan of "Vietnamization."

Under Vietnamization, more responsibility for fighting the war would be turned over to the South Vietnamese forces. Gradually, American troops would be withdrawn. Then, with the United States cheering on the troops from the sidelines, the South Vietnamese would be free to defeat the North Vietnamese on their own.

The Vietnamization strategy never really had much chance of success. The South Vietnamese government was too corrupt, and the South Vietnamese Army was too weak to fight well without the help of better trained, better equipped American soldiers. In April 1970, Nixon ordered American troops into eastern Cambodia to attack North Vietnamese forces. Most of the North Vietnamese withdrew without a fight. This invasion succeeded only in making an already unstable political situation in Cambodia even worse. It would lead to the Communist takeover of that country by the fanatical Pol Pot and his Khmer Rouge. Pol Pot would go on to murder up to one million of his countrymen in the "killing fields" of Cambodia. Nixon's invasion of Cambodia would also lead to tragic events much closer to home.

Photo credit: www.ronkimballstock.com H44170 © Highsmith LLC 2003

Lotus

A War Ac̶̶̶̶̶dents

On Apri̶̶̶̶̶ ̶̶̶̶̶ ̶̶̶̶̶ announced the American
invasio̶̶̶̶̶ ̶̶̶̶̶ ̶̶̶̶̶protests erupted at college
camp̶̶̶̶̶ ̶̶̶̶̶ ̶̶̶̶̶traged students cried out for
pea̶̶̶̶̶ ̶̶̶̶̶e response to the students was
fa̶̶̶̶̶ ̶̶̶̶̶tate University in Ohio, the Ohio
̶̶̶̶̶ ̶̶̶̶̶ on the unarmed students, killing
̶̶̶̶̶. And at Jackson State College in
̶̶̶̶̶d state troopers killed two students.
̶̶̶̶̶ed by these events, and opposition to
̶̶̶̶̶ger than ever.

A student
(above) lies
on the ground
after National
Guardsmen
opened fire
on a crowd of
demonstrators
at Kent State
University on
May 4, 1970.

Giving Young People the Vote

The post-World War II baby boom had created a huge population of young people in the 1960s and 1970s. Throughout the Vietnam War, these young people had made their voices heard by protesting the war and by advocating new ideals for society. But until 1971, many of these young political activists could not even vote unless they were over the age of twenty-one. Partly because of the outspoken attitude of American youth during this period, and partly in an effort to give young people the opportunity to fight for changes through the ballot box rather than violence, the Twenty-sixth Amendment to the Constitution was ratified in the summer of 1971, lowering the national voting age to eighteen. From then on, even teens would have a chance to help elect their government representatives.

Ending the Vietnam War

In February 1970, National Security Advisor Henry Kissinger had begun secret negotiations aimed at ending the Vietnam War with the North Vietnamese. By 1972, the talks, no longer secret, were continuing—as was the war. But it seemed as though progress was being made. The number of American troops in Vietnam was steadily decreasing. Hoping to win another term in office in the 1972 election, Nixon wanted to be seen as a peacemaker. In February of that year, Nixon became the first American president to visit China. In May, he became the first United States president to visit the Soviet Union. While he was there, he signed nuclear weapons treaties. Nixon seemed to be doing all the right things. In November, American voters handed Nixon a landslide re-election victory over George McGovern.

President Nixon
and his wife,
Pat, visit the
Great Wall
during Nixon's
historic visit to
China in 1972.

In December, the peace talks with the North Vietnamese broke down. Nixon ordered a massive bombing of North Vietnam. By January 1973, the peace talks were on again, and on January 27, an agreement was signed. By March 29, 1973, the last American troops had left South Vietnam. The war continued without the help of American soldiers. By April 1975, when Saigon, the South Vietnamese capital, fell to North Vietnam, all American advisors and other personnel had left South Vietnam. The Vietnam War quickly ended when North Vietnam took over South Vietnam.

Watergate

On June 17, 1972, five men were arrested for breaking into the Democratic National Committee headquarters at the Watergate hotel-office complex in Washington, D.C. Two reporters for the *Washington Post*, Carl Bernstein and Bob Woodward, began covering the story. They traced connections between the burglars and President Nixon's re-election committee largely through an anonymous source known only as "Deep Throat." They published reports about their progress. Eventually, their work would lead to televised hearings of the Senate Watergate Committee in 1973. All of Nixon's top advisors had to testify. Each had played a role in the scandal, and evidence pointed to Nixon's involvement in authorizing a cover-up of the illegal break-in. High administration officials, including Attorney General John Mitchell, Special Counsel John Dean, Chief of Staff H. R. Haldeman, and Domestic Advisor John Ehrlichman, were sentenced to prison terms.

The Watergate affair revealed a shocking degree of corruption in the Nixon administration. In a separate scandal, Vice President Spiro Agnew was forced to resign in 1973. He was accused of accepting bribes and kickbacks while serving as governor of Maryland, and he was charged with federal income tax evasion. Gerald Ford was appointed vice president to replace Agnew.

In May 1973, Archibald Cox was appointed special prosecutor to investigate the Watergate affair. As other presidents had done in the past, Nixon had secretly taped conversations that took place in the White House. When Cox ordered Nixon to turn over the tapes, Nixon had Cox fired. Acting Attorney General Robert Bork then appointed Leon Jaworski as Cox's replacement.

In July 1974, the Supreme Court ordered Nixon to turn over the tapes to the special prosecutor. The tapes proved that Nixon had lied about the cover-up. He now faced impeachment. On August 8, he announced his decision to resign the presidency. The next day, Vice President Gerald Ford became president. On September 8, Ford granted Nixon a pardon for any crimes he might have committed while in office. Ford's popularity in opinion polls immediately dropped from 71 percent to 49 percent.

In May 2005, after more than thirty years of anonymity, "Deep Throat" finally revealed himself to be former FBI official W. Mark Felt (above).

The ERA

There were, of course, issues that mattered to people besides Watergate. One of the most important was the women's rights movement. Women wanted to have the same kinds of job opportunities as men did and they wanted equal pay for equal work. At the beginning of the decade, women earned about 57 percent of what men earned for the same work. Feminists came to believe that a new law that would protect women's rights and end discrimination had become necessary.

The struggle for congressional passage and ratification of the Equal Rights Amendment (ERA) was led by the National Organization for Women (NOW). The ERA stated: "Equality of rights under the law shall not be denied or abridged by the United States or by any state on account of sex." Congress passed the ERA in 1972, but in order to become part of the Constitution it also had to be ratified, or approved, by three fourths of the states. Ultimately, the ERA went down in defeat.

The Right to Choose

A major milestone in women's rights involved the issue of abortion. In 1973, the United States Supreme Court, in *Roe* v. *Wade*, ruled that laws prohibiting abortion violated a woman's right of privacy. This proved to be a very controversial ruling, and both then and now, people have debated the issue.

The Peanut Farmer Who Became President

The presidential election in 1976 was a close race between Gerald Ford and Jimmy Carter, a peanut farmer from Georgia. Both men appealed to voters as basically nice, decent, honest

When President Carter (below) was elected in 1976, it was obvious that Americans were looking for a change.

men—a welcome contrast to Nixon and his administration. Carter won the election.

Carter tried to get Americans to face a harsh new economic reality. He said that, because there were limits to available energy resources in the world, energy costs would become increasingly more expensive. Carter asked Americans to save energy wherever possible. To set a good example, Carter announced that he was keeping the White House thermostat at 68°F. Carter would often appear on television in the White House, wearing a thick sweater to show that he was saving energy by using less heat. Carter's message did not go over very well with Americans.

The Panama Canal Treaty

President Carter was unpopular with many Americans because of the poor economic conditions that reigned during his administration. He did, however, have some significant achievements during his term as president. Among them was the Panama Canal Treaty of 1977.

Since 1914, when the canal was completed by American construction crews, the United States had run the Panama Canal. Over time, the local people of Panama came to resent the United States presence. They began to protest, demanding that the Panama Canal Zone (where the canal is located) be returned to Panama. As unrest grew worse in the 1970s, President Carter decided to take action. In 1977, Carter and Panamanian head of state Omar Torrijos Herrera signed a treaty. It provided for the return of the canal to Panama on December 31, 1999. The agreement met with mixed reactions. Some Americans were angry to lose such an important possession. Others, however, considered it a diplomatic triumph for Carter.

Stagflation

To make matters worse, there was a new problem in the American economy. Inflation (rising prices for items) combined with high unemployment and a stagnant economy to create what was called "stagflation." Partly due to the higher cost of oil and other resources, the economy was no longer growing as rapidly as it had been in earlier years. In addition, the size of the workforce had increased tremendously, to some degree because more women were looking for jobs outside the home. With so many people needing jobs, the economy could not grow fast enough to make room for everyone. As a result, there was widespread unemployment.

OPEC and the Oil Crisis

Because America was so dependent on foreign oil, Americans faced a serious fuel problem. During the 1970s, gasoline prices skyrocketed, partly because of the crisis in the Middle East. Angry that Western nations like the United States supported

One of President Carter's biggest diplomatic achievements was the 1977 Panama Canal Treaty, which provided for the return of the Panama Canal (above) to Panama by the end of 1999.

Israel in its war against its Arab neighbors, the Arab nations of the Oil Producing and Exporting Countries (OPEC) started an oil embargo. They forced Americans to pay very high prices in order to buy the oil needed to run cars and other machinery. As a result, Americans had to deal with high gas prices and very long lines at the gas pump.

For many years, Americans had enjoyed driving their big cars, known as "gas guzzlers." When the price of gasoline shot up to the seemingly astronomical price of more than a dollar a gallon, many Americans looked for ways to make driving more economical. The compact cars of foreign auto manufacturers—Japanese and German—became very popular with American consumers. The "Big Three" American auto-makers—Ford, General Motors, and Chrysler—scrambled to produce their own version of the compact car. More than a quarter of a million Americans bought the new motorized bicycle known as a moped. The Department of Transportation had approved the use of mopeds in 1973. The moped was a truly economical means of transportation, capable of getting 150 miles to a gallon of gas.

To help ease its reliance on foreign oil, the United States authorized the development of oil fields on Alaska's Arctic coast. The huge Prudhoe Bay oil field is the largest in North America. Oil began flowing through the 800-mile Trans-Alaska Pipeline once the three-year project was completed in 1977.

The Camp David Accords

The Middle East had been a hotbed of problems for decades, as Arabs fought Israel over what both groups considered holy land. On October 6, 1973, Egypt and Syria carried out a surprise attack on Israel on the holiest day of the Jewish

calendar—Yom Kippur, the Day of Atonement. Israel won the war, but it suffered heavy losses, because it had not been sufficiently prepared.

In 1977, Egyptian President Anwar Sadat decided that the time had come to make peace with Israel. He made a historic visit to Jerusalem to meet with Israeli Prime Minister Menachem Begin. Jimmy Carter then invited both leaders to come to Camp David, the presidential retreat in Maryland, where he offered to help them reach a peace agreement.

President Carter is also remembered for negotiating the Camp David Accords between Egypt's Anwar Sadat (above left) and Israel's Menachem Begin.

Militant Muslim protesters demonstrate outside of the U.S. Embassy in Tehran, Iran, on November 8, 1979.

Carter helped Sadat and Begin overcome numerous obstacles in their negotiations. The final peace agreement was signed in March 1979. Known as the Camp David Accords, this peace agreement was Jimmy Carter's greatest foreign policy triumph.

The Ayatollah Khomeini

In November 1979, a crisis erupted in a different part of the Middle East—Iran. An Islamic revolution had swept the country early in 1979. In January, the Shah of Iran, who had been an ally of the United States, was overthrown and forced to flee. The Ayatollah Ruhollah Khomeini, the spiritual and political leader of the revolutionaries, returned to Iran in triumph.

In November, Iranian students who supported the Ayatollah seized the American Embassy in Tehran and took sixty-two Americans hostage. The students were angry because the Shah was being treated for cancer in a hospital in the United States.

Throughout the next year, television viewers around the world watched the American captives being paraded before jeering crowds. The Iranians burned American flags and chanted anti-American slogans. By November 1980, fifty-two hostages were still being held. This situation proved to be a disaster for the Carter administration, which seemed unable to end the crisis, and was one major cause of Carter's defeat in the 1980 presidential election.

Three Mile Island

Throughout the 1970s, disaster films about natural or man-made catastrophes were very popular in America. Movies such as *The Poseidon Adventure*, *The Towering Inferno*, and *Earthquake* provided hours of escape from real-world disasters, such as the war in Vietnam.

Most people considered the events portrayed in disaster movies far-fetched, especially those in *The China Syndrome*, a 1979 film about an accident at a nuclear power plant. But on March 28, 1979, shortly after that film's release, the country had a real-life disaster that was as scary as anything on the big screen. Engineers at the Three Mile Island nuclear power plant in Pennsylvania noticed a mechanical problem with the cooling system. They shut off the water to the reactor. Without water to keep it cool, the reactor quickly heated up and began to melt. Radiation began to leak outside. For a while, it looked as if a total meltdown might occur. Luckily, engineers were able to cool down the reactor. Still, there was great concern for the health of local residents, despite government claims that the radiation released did not pose a threat.

Major antinuclear demonstrations were held after Three Mile Island. The result was a limit on the use and further construction of nuclear power plants, as well as a fear of nuclear accidents that continues even today.

Love Canal

Nuclear power plants were not the only source of potential environmental disasters. In the mid-1970s, residents in the Love Canal area of Niagara Falls, New York, began to notice chemical smells and strangely colored water seeping out of the ground. Chemicals began bubbling up in lawns and basements. The residents of Love Canal had a much higher rate of cancer and other diseases than did people in other

The cooling towers of Three Mile Island's Unit 2 reactor (below left) and the towers of Unit 1 (below right). The Unit 2 reactor has remained unused since the 1979 accident.

neighborhoods. The Love Canal neighborhood was built on an area that in the 1930s and 1940s had been used by Hooker Chemical Company to dump toxic chemical wastes. Among these wastes was dioxin, one of the most toxic substances ever created. In July 1978, President Jimmy Carter declared Love Canal a federal disaster area. Fifteen million dollars was set aside for the relocation of Love Canal families. Sadly, there were about 50,000 other toxic waste disposal sites all across America. There was now a new law mandating safe disposal of toxic wastes, but this came too late to help families living near these sites.

Earth Day

This new awareness of the environment and the dangers that could be caused by pollution and waste helped create a new holiday. In April 1970, the first Earth Day celebration was held. It began as an effort to make all people take notice of the harm human beings have done to the environment throughout their history, and to look at ways pollution and other problems can be corrected or prevented.

Over 20,000 gathered at Philadelphia's Fairmount Park on April 23, 1970, to celebrate Earth Day (right).

The EPA

The idea of "returning to nature" became very popular in the 1970s. Aside from influencing art and lifestyles, it had an effect on government policy. In 1970, the Environmental Protection Agency (EPA) was created. It was set up to establish standards to prevent pollution from automobiles and industry, and to protect Americans from the dangers of toxic chemicals and radioactive waste. It made the new outlook of taking care of nature an official part of the government.

The Apollo-Soyuz mission of 1975 was one of the first times the United States and Soviet Union cooperated in a joint scientific project.

Space Exploration

Important milestones in the exploration of the solar system were achieved during the 1970s. Following the historic landing on the moon in 1969 by the astronauts of Apollo 11, NASA launched several more successful moon landings, ending with Apollo 17 in 1972. In 1975, the United States and the Soviet Union, in a rare show of superpower cooperation, linked together an Apollo spacecraft with a Soviet Soyuz spacecraft for forty-four hours to form a temporary orbiting space station. Television viewers on Earth were able to watch as American astronauts and Russian cosmonauts visited each other.

Unmanned spacecrafts were launched to many different parts of the solar system. The Mariner, Voyager, Viking, and Pioneer space probes sent information back to Earth from Mercury, Venus, Mars, Jupiter, and Saturn. In 1976, Viking I and Viking 2 orbited Mars. When the Viking landing crafts reached the surface of Mars, they began sending back amazingly clear full-color pictures of the rocky, desertlike Martian landscape. It was like a science-fiction story come true. The Viking landers also tested samples of Martian soil. Unfortunately, unlike science fiction, the Viking mission found no signs of Martian life.

The 1970s also featured several important explorations of other planets, such as Mars, Saturn (below), and Jupiter.

In May 1973, another important event took place for the American space program. *Skylab*, the United States' first space station, was launched. *Skylab* was designed to orbit, or move

around, Earth at a distance of three hundred miles. Aboard the space station were astronauts, who conducted scientific and medical experiments. *Skylab* was manned by three research crews before the astronauts left the space station and returned to Earth in February 1974. *Skylab* was supposed to be able to continue to send information back to Earth, to help NASA continue its space research for many years to come. In 1979, however, *Skylab*'s orbit began to deteriorate. In July of that year, parts of the space station crashed in parts of Australia and in the Indian Ocean. Fortunately, no one was hurt. But the possibility of using *Skylab* to continue space exploration was over.

A Hole in the Ozone Layer

Science also gave the world some not-so-good news in the 1970s. In 1974, scientists announced that gases, known as chlorofluorocarbons, or CFCs, which are given off by aerosol spray cans and other everyday items, were harmful to the ozone layer. The ozone layer of the atmosphere protects the earth from deadly ultraviolet radiation from the sun. The study predicted that further damage to the ozone layer could cause changes in the earth's weather as well as increases in the number of skin cancer cases.

The launch of Skylab (above) brought hope for many different kinds of future research.

The Computer in the Garage

Until the 1970s, computers were so expensive that only the largest corporations and government agencies could afford them. They were also so big that they occupied entire rooms. In 1976, Steve Jobs and Steve Wozniak, two college dropouts,

Steve Jobs (below) introduces his new Apple II computer in 1977.

went to work in a garage and produced the Apple I, a crude version of a personal computer (PC). In 1977, they began selling a better version, the Apple II. People snapped up the Apples as quickly as they could be built.

At the same time, Bill Gates, another college dropout, founded Microsoft with his partner, Paul Allen. Bill Gates had developed an operating system for IBM to be used on the IBM PC. His new company, Microsoft, which developed and sold PC operating system software, would eventually become America's biggest corporation—and Bill Gates would become America's richest man.

Overcoming Infertility

The 1970s also saw great breakthroughs in medicine. Until 1978, a woman with blocked Fallopian tubes could not become pregnant. But in that year, Louise Brown, the world's first test-tube baby, was born in Oldham, England. An egg was taken from Louise's mother and placed in a

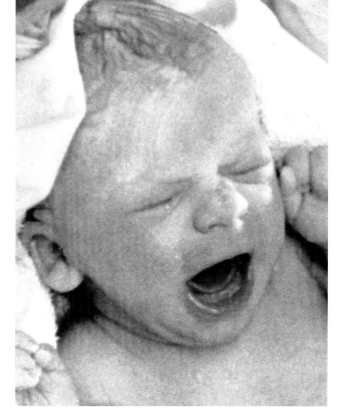

Petri dish. There, the egg was fertilized with Louise's father's sperm. When the fertilized egg had developed into an eight-celled embryo, it was implanted in the mother's uterus. A normal development of the fetus followed. Eventually, healthy five-pound, twelve-ounce Louise was born.

The resignation of President Nixon (below) after the Watergate scandal was just one of the many unforgettable events that marked the 1970s.

An Amazing Decade

The 1970s were marked by several serious crises. Among them were the Watergate scandal, unrest in the Middle East, and the Vietnam War. These problems in the United States and around the world made the 1970s a time of upheaval and dissatisfaction with the way society and government worked. People seemed to be disgusted with politics and government and sought to escape traditional ways of life. Because of this desire for change, the 1970s were also marked by unusual fads and fashions, from the pet rock to disco. From the political awareness inspired by opposition to the Vietnam War to the bell-bottoms and designer jeans of the fashion world—the 1970s were a decade that has continually shown its influence and will probably do so for many years to come.

Timeline

1970 Musicians **Jimi Hendrix** and **Janis Joplin** die; **President Richard Nixon** orders bombing of Cambodia; **Kent State** shootings occur; EPA created; First **Earth Day** celebrated.

1971 **Jim Morrison**, lead singer of the Doors, dies; **Twenty-sixth Amendment**, giving eighteen-year-olds the right to vote, is ratified.

1972 AIM seizes Bureau of Indian Affairs; **Gloria Steinem** publishes first issue of *Ms.*; Congress passes **ERA**, but it fails to be ratified; **Watergate** break-in occurs; **Richard Nixon** wins re-election to the presidency; Massacre of Israeli athletes at the **Olympic Games** committed by Arab terrorists.

1973 AIM holds a protest against unfair treatment of Indians at Wounded Knee; **Billie Jean King** wins the U.S. Open and defeats **Bobby Riggs** in the "Battle of the Sexes"; *Roe* v. *Wade* decision protects the right to abortion; **CB radios** become popular; **Billie Jean King** helps form the Women's Tennis Association; United States troops pull out of Vietnam; Senate Watergate Committee hearings are televised; **Vice President Spiro Agnew** resigns; Egypt and Syria attack Israel in Yom Kippur War; *Skylab* is launched.

1974 Indian Self-Determination Act passed; **Cass Elliott** of the Mamas and the Papas dies; **Muhammad Ali** defeats **George Foreman** in "The Rumble in the Jungle"; **President Richard Nixon** resigns; **Gerald Ford** becomes president; CFCs are found to be harmful to the ozone layer.

1975   Mood ring goes on sale; **Pet rock** becomes available; **Muhammad Ali** defeats **Joe Frazier** in "The Thrilla in Manila"; United States and Soviet Union link an Apollo spacecraft with a Soviet Soyuz spacecraft; **Arthur Ashe** becomes first African American to win Wimbledon tennis tournament; **Evel Knievel** leaps fourteen Greyhound buses on his motorcycle.

1976   Writer **Tom Wolfe** describes the 1970s as the "Me Decade"; *Rocky* opens in theaters; **Jimmy Carter** is elected president; *Viking 1* and *Viking 2* orbit Mars; **Steve Jobs** and **Steve Wozniak** develop the Apple I.

1977   *Roots* miniseries premieres; *Saturday Night Fever* comes out in theaters; *Star Wars* premieres; **Elvis Presley** dies; **President Carter** signs **Panama Canal Treaty**; **Steve Wozniak** and **Steve Jobs** begin selling the Apple II.

1978   In Jonestown, People's Temple cult members led by **Reverend Jim Jones** commit mass suicide; *Grease* opens in theaters; *Superman: The Movie* premieres; The disco craze reaches its height; First test-tube baby is born.

1979   **Cesar Chavez** leads strike for United Farm Workers Union; **Three Mile Island** disaster occurs; **Camp David Accords** between Egypt and Israel are signed; **Ayatollah Khomeini** comes to power in Iran after overthrowing the Shah; Americans are taken hostage in Iran.

Further Reading

Books

Duden, Jane. *1970s*. Morristown, N.J.: Silver Burdett Press, 1989.

Fremon, David K. *The Watergate Scandal in American History*. Springfield, N.J.: Enslow Publishers, Inc., 1998.

Hopkinson, C. *Twentieth Century*. Tulsa, Okla.: EDC Publishing, 1994.

Jennings, Peter, and Todd Brewster. *The Century*. New York: Doubleday, 1998.

Junior Chronicle of the 20th Century. New York: DK Publishing, Inc., 1997.

McCormick, Anita Louise. *The Vietnam Antiwar Movement in American History*. Berkeley Heights, N.J.: Enslow Publishers, Inc., 2000.

Time-Life Books editors. *Time of Transition: The 70s*. Richmond, Va.: Time-Life, Inc., 1998.

Internet Addresses

Nixon and Watergate
http://www.archives.gov/exhibits/american_originals/nixon.html

70's Preservation Society
http://www.70ps.com/

Jimmy Carter: Thirty-Ninth President, 1977–1981
http://www.whitehouse.gov/history/presidents/jc39.html

Index

DATE DUE